PLANET EARTH

by Matt Mullins

CHERRY LAKE PUBLISHING • ANN ARBOR, MICHIGAN

A NOTE TO PARENTS AND TEACHERS: Please review the instructions for these experiments before your children do them. Be sure to help them with any experiments you do not think they can safely conduct on their own.

A NOTE TO KIDS: Be sure to ask an adult for help with these experiments when you need it. Always put your safety first!

Published in the United States of America by
Cherry Lake Publishing
Ann Arbor, Michigan
www.cherrylakepublishing.com

Content Editor: Robert Wolffe, EdD,
Professor of Teacher Education,
Bradley University, Peoria, Illinois

Book design and illustration: The Design Lab

Photo Credits: Cover and page 1, ©Mashe/Dreamstime.com; pages 4 and 11, Photo courtesy of NASA; page 7, ©jan kranendonk, used under license from Shutterstock, Inc.; page 10, ©Jeff R. Clow, used under license from Shutterstock, Inc.; page 16, ©Jgroup/Dreamstime.com; page 20, ©Juliengrondin/Dreamstime.com; page 29, ©Elegeyda/Dreamstime.com

Library of Congress Cataloging-in-Publication Data
Mullins, Matt.
Super cool science experiments: Planet Earth / by Matt Mullins.
p. cm.—(Science explorer)
Includes bibliographical references and index.
ISBN-13: 978-1-60279-515-0 ISBN-10: 1-60279-515-0 (lib. bdg.)
ISBN-13: 978-1-60279-605-8 ISBN-10: 1-60279-605-X (pbk.)
1. Earth—Experiments—Juvenile literature. 2. Geophysics—Experiments—Juvenile literature. I. Title.
II. Title: Planet Earth. III. Series.
QB631.4.M85 2010
550.78—dc22 2009011183

Cherry Lake Publishing would like to acknowledge the work of The Partnership for 21st Century Skills. Please visit *www.21stcenturyskills.org* for more information.

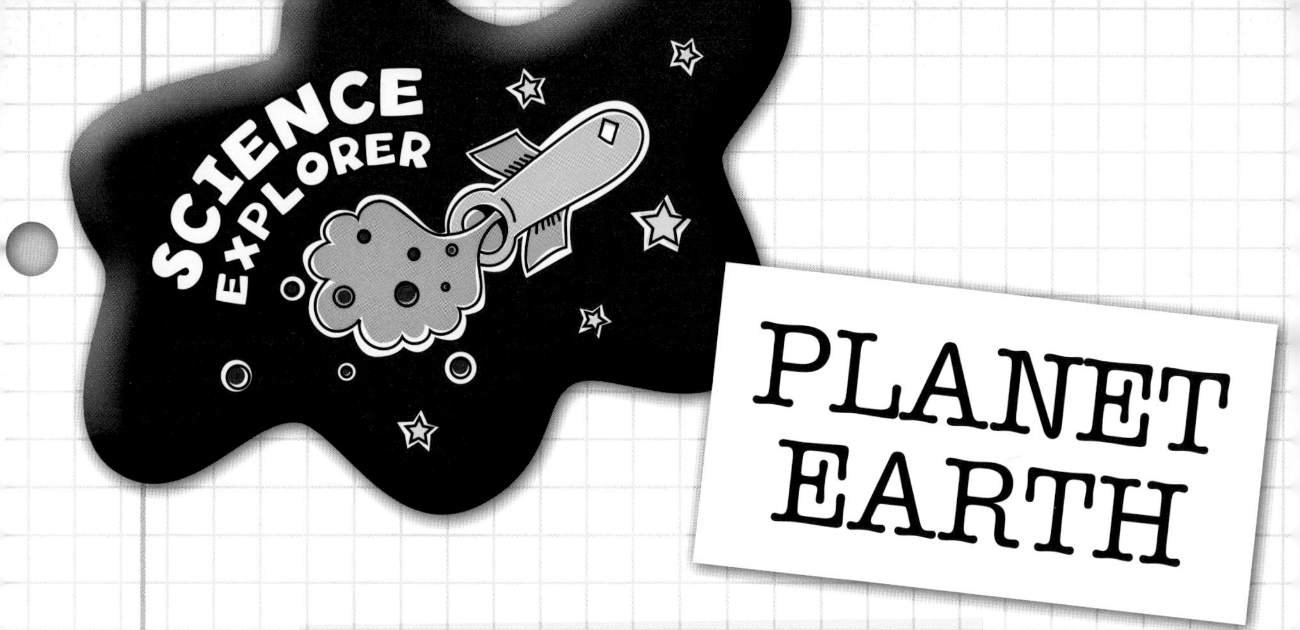

PLANET EARTH

TABLE OF CONTENTS

Our Big, Round Home

What's big and round and blue all over? Our home, the planet Earth! When you live somewhere as full of variety as Earth, you need all kinds of scientists to study it.

Maybe you've wondered how Earth changes. Or how its many parts work together. If so, you are on your way to thinking like an earth scientist. In this book, we'll learn how scientists think. We'll run fun experiments about planet Earth. You'll even learn how to design your own experiments!

There is always something new to discover about our amazing home planet!

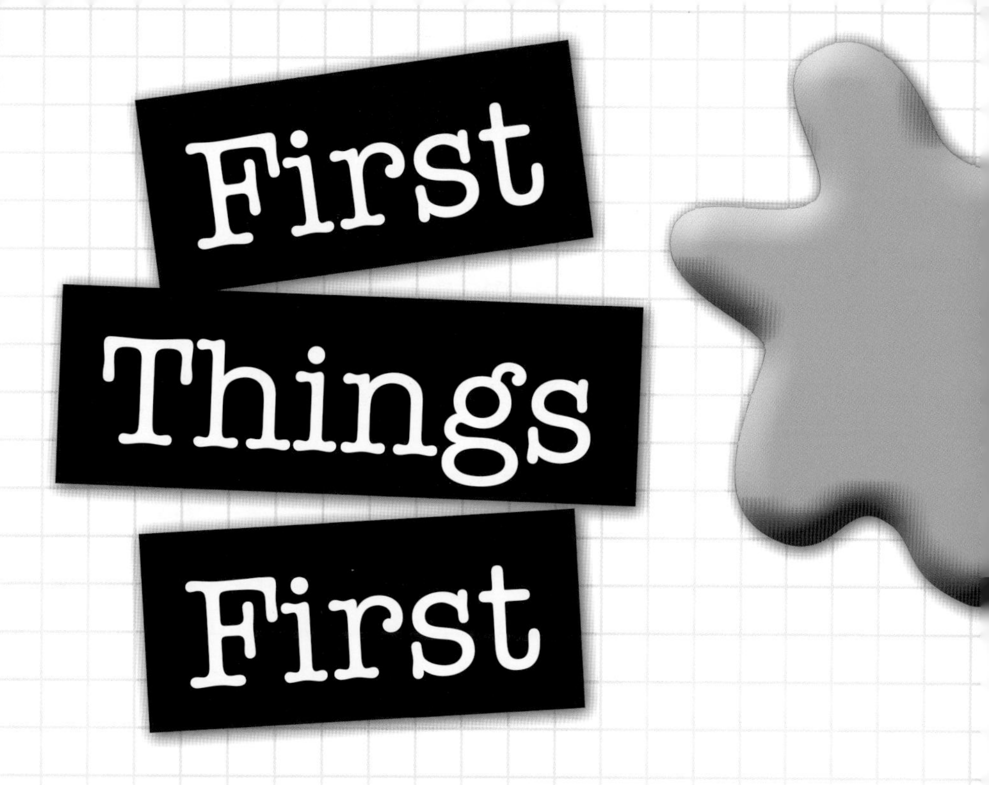

First Things First

Scientists learn about Earth by studying everything about it. Astronomers study the stars, space, and Earth's relationship to the rest of the solar system. Volcanologists study volcanoes and eruptions. Climatologists study the atmosphere and weather patterns. The list of scientists who study Earth goes on and on.

Good scientists take notes on everything they discover. They write down their observations and think about what it all means. When scientists design experiments, they must think very clearly. The way they think about problems is often called the scientific method. What is the scientific method? It's a step-by-step way of finding answers to specific questions. The steps don't always follow the same pattern. Sometimes scientists change their minds. The process often works something like this:

scientific method

- **Step One:** A scientist gathers the facts and makes observations about one particular thing.
- **Step Two:** The scientist comes up with a question that is not answered by all the observations and facts.
- **Step Three:** The scientist creates a hypothesis. This is a statement of what the scientist thinks is probably the answer to the question.
- **Step Four:** The scientist tests the hypothesis. He or she designs an experiment to see whether the hypothesis is correct. The scientist does the experiment and writes down what happens.
- **Step Five:** The scientist draws a conclusion based on how the experiment turned out. The conclusion might be that the hypothesis is correct. Sometimes, though, the hypothesis is not correct. In that case, the scientist might develop a new hypothesis and another experiment.

You will use the scientific method as you do the experiments in this book. You'll observe Earth and the moon, how oceans help keep temperatures stable, and how the air we breathe has weight. You'll develop hypotheses, test them, and draw conclusions. In other words, you'll think like a scientist. Ready? Let's get going!

Experiment #1
Earth Is a Sphere

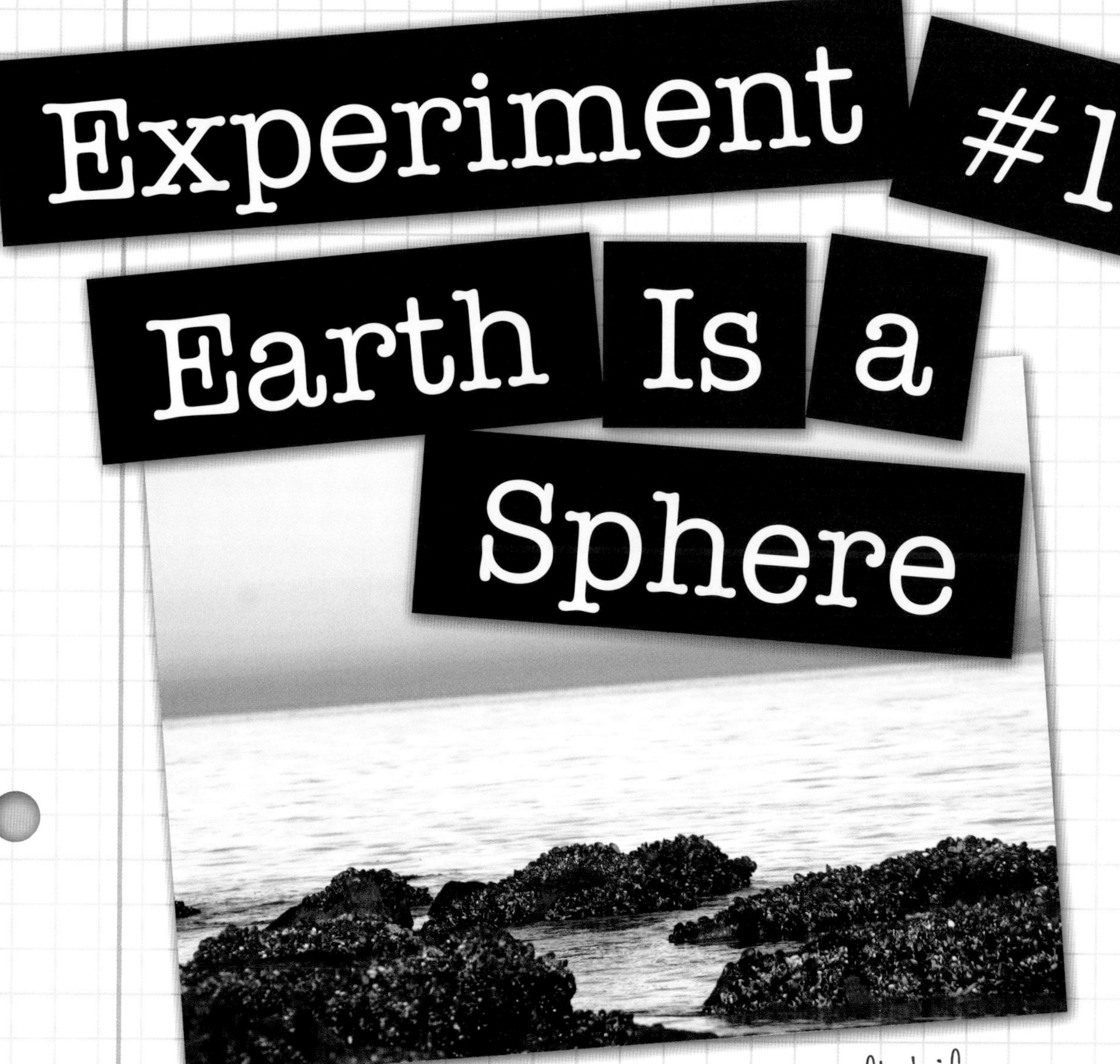

You might think Earth is flat if you are standing on its surface.

For thousands of years, people wondered about Earth's shape. Some even thought it was flat. In fact, Earth is a sphere—a giant ball.

More than 2,000 years ago, the Greek philosopher Aristotle observed evidence for a sphere-shaped Earth. He saw an eclipse of the moon. Earth was between the sun and the moon. This caused a shadow to fall on the moon. Aristotle believed that only a sphere could cast the kinds of curved shadows he saw. Is this true? What do you think? Come up with a hypothesis. Here is one option: **Only a sphere always casts a round shadow.**

Here's what you'll need:

- Dark room
- Lamp without its shade
- Table
- Small box
- Clean, empty soup can
- Frisbee
- Ball

Gather all your materials before you begin.

Instructions:

1. Find a room that blocks outside light. A room without windows works well. So does a room with windows that have thick drapes or blinds that you can close. Set up a lamp on a table several feet away from a wall. Turn off the lights in the room.
2. Turn on the lamp. Stand between the lamp and the wall. Hold the box out on your hand, and position

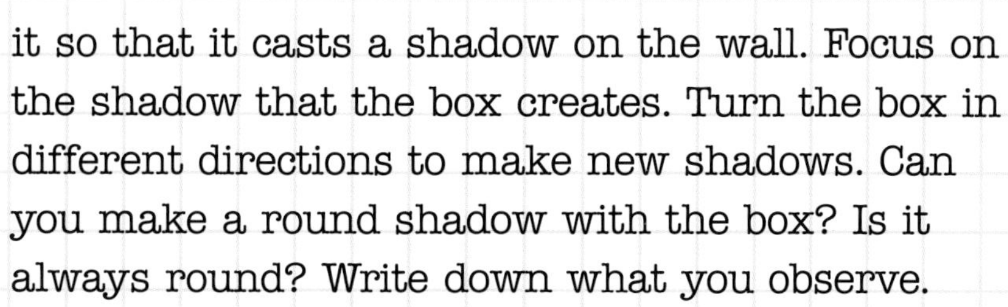

it so that it casts a shadow on the wall. Focus on the shadow that the box creates. Turn the box in different directions to make new shadows. Can you make a round shadow with the box? Is it always round? Write down what you observe.

3. In the same way, use the soup can to create shadows. Turn it, and make as many different shadows as you can. Are the shadows always round? Can you make a rectangular shadow with the can by holding it horizontally?
4. Test the Frisbee. What kinds of shadows can you make? Are some of them not round?
5. Test the ball. Turn it in every direction you can think of. Are the shadows always round?

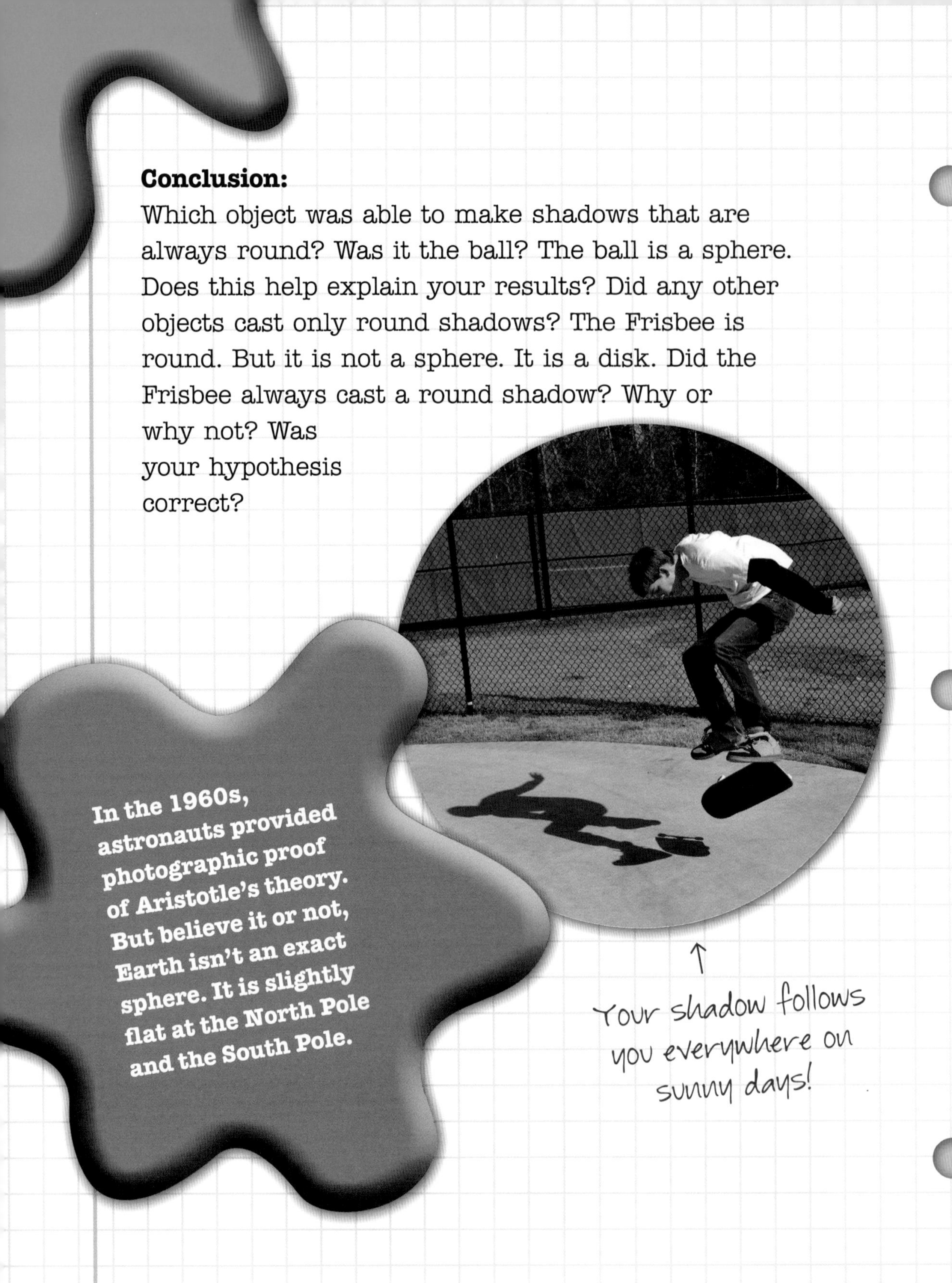

Conclusion:

Which object was able to make shadows that are always round? Was it the ball? The ball is a sphere. Does this help explain your results? Did any other objects cast only round shadows? The Frisbee is round. But it is not a sphere. It is a disk. Did the Frisbee always cast a round shadow? Why or why not? Was your hypothesis correct?

In the 1960s, astronauts provided photographic proof of Aristotle's theory. But believe it or not, Earth isn't an exact sphere. It is slightly flat at the North Pole and the South Pole.

Your shadow follows you everywhere on sunny days!

Experiment #2 Earth, the Sun, and the Moon

You know that Earth is not alone in space. It is the third of eight planets that circle a big star in our solar system. Earth spins, or rotates, around its axis as it orbits the sun. It takes exactly 1 year for Earth to zoom around this star.

The moon circles Earth just as Earth circles the sun. The moon is so big and heavy and close that it creates, like the sun does, a pull on Earth. We call this pull gravity. The moon isn't nearly as large as the sun. The sun's gravitational pull is much stronger than the moon's.

You have probably noticed that the sun is very bright. It's not safe to look directly at the sun. You would hurt your eyes. So how do scientists study it? Experts study the sun (and the moon) using many different tools. They look through telescopes, send out radio waves, and take pictures from satellites. Different tools have helped scientists determine the diameter—the width of a circle or sphere—of the sun and moon. The sun is 1,392,000 kilometers (864,949 miles) in diameter. The moon is 3,474 kilometers (2,159 mi) in diameter.

You probably don't have a powerful telescope or satellite at home. But could we make our own tool for observing the sun and moon? A pinhole camera is a simple device in which light passes through a tiny hole into a darkened box. Could a pinhole camera help us determine the diameters of the sun and moon? Come up with a hypothesis. Here is one option: **A pinhole camera can be used as a tool to measure the sun's and moon's diameters.**

Here's what you'll need:

- Large cardboard box
- Box cutter
- Scissors
- Aluminum foil
- Tape
- Pin
- White paper
- Pencil
- Ruler or tape measure
- Notebook paper
- Calculator

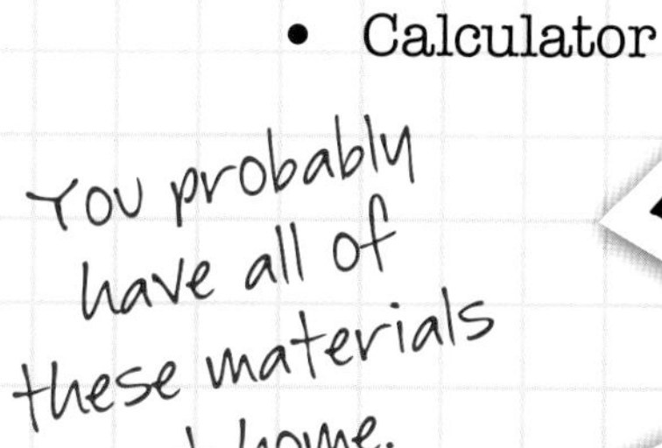

You probably have all of these materials at home.

Instructions:

1. Have an adult help you cut a square into 1 side of the box with the box cutter. The square should be 3/4 inch by 3/4 inch (1.9 centimeters by 1.9 cm).
2. Use scissors to cut a square of aluminum foil, and tape it over the hole. It should completely cover the hole.
3. Push the point of a pin through the center of the foil. Now you have a pinhole camera!

4. Tape a piece of white paper inside the box on the side opposite the pinhole.
5. Stand outside in a sunny spot. Turn your back to the sun. Put the box over your head so that you're looking at the white paper. You may have to take some time to adjust the box so that you don't block the pinhole.
6. Have someone hold the box in place once you find the correct setup. You should see an image of the sun shining on the white paper. Mark the paper with a pencil along both sides of the image.
7. Take the box off your head. Use the ruler or tape measure to measure the distance between the pinhole and the white paper. Then measure the distance in centimeters between your pencil marks. Write down the numbers on a piece of paper.
8. To determine the diameter of the sun, you need to know that the distance of Earth from the sun is 149,600,000 kilometers. Use a calculator and follow these steps:
   (a) Divide the diameter of the image of the sun by the distance from the pinhole to the sheet of paper.

No, this is not my new hat!

(b) Take the number you come up with and multiply it by the distance from Earth to the sun.

(c) The number you come up with is the diameter of the sun in kilometers. Write down your answer.

On a clear night with a bright, full moon, you can confirm the moon's diameter in the same way. For your calculation, you'll need to know that the distance from Earth to the moon is 384,000 kilometers. Repeat the steps you used to confirm the sun's diameter. Record your answer.

Conclusion:

What number did you get for the diameter of the sun? Was it close to 1,392,000 kilometers? What number did you get for the diameter of the moon? Was it close to 3,474 kilometers? Was your pinhole camera a good tool for confirming the diameters? Was your hypothesis correct?

The sun and the moon are made of totally different matter. The sun is a ball of burning gas. The moon is solid rock. The moon looks bright because it reflects sunlight like a mirror.

Experiment #3 Water Keeps Earth Just Right

It isn't easy to survive in the desert.

We need the oceans to survive. One of the most important things the oceans do for Earth is keep temperatures stable. But how? Think about a desert, where there is little water. It gets very hot during the day, but cold at night. Soil and rock absorb heat from the sun. But do they hold on to that heat very well? Could water have the ability to retain, or hold on to, heat better than those materials? Could that be a reason behind water's role in regulating the climate? Come up with a hypothesis about water and heat. Here is one possibility: **Water retains and manages heat better than soil.**

Here's what you'll need:

- 3 identical, clean aluminum cans
- Kitchen scale
- Garden soil
- Sand
- Water
- Plastic wrap
- Thermometer
- Sheet of cardboard
- Black cloth
- Cookie sheet
- Oven
- Oven mitts
- Hot pads

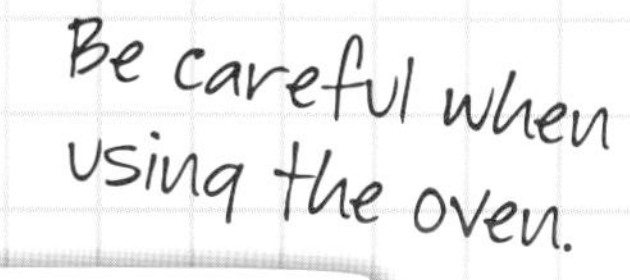

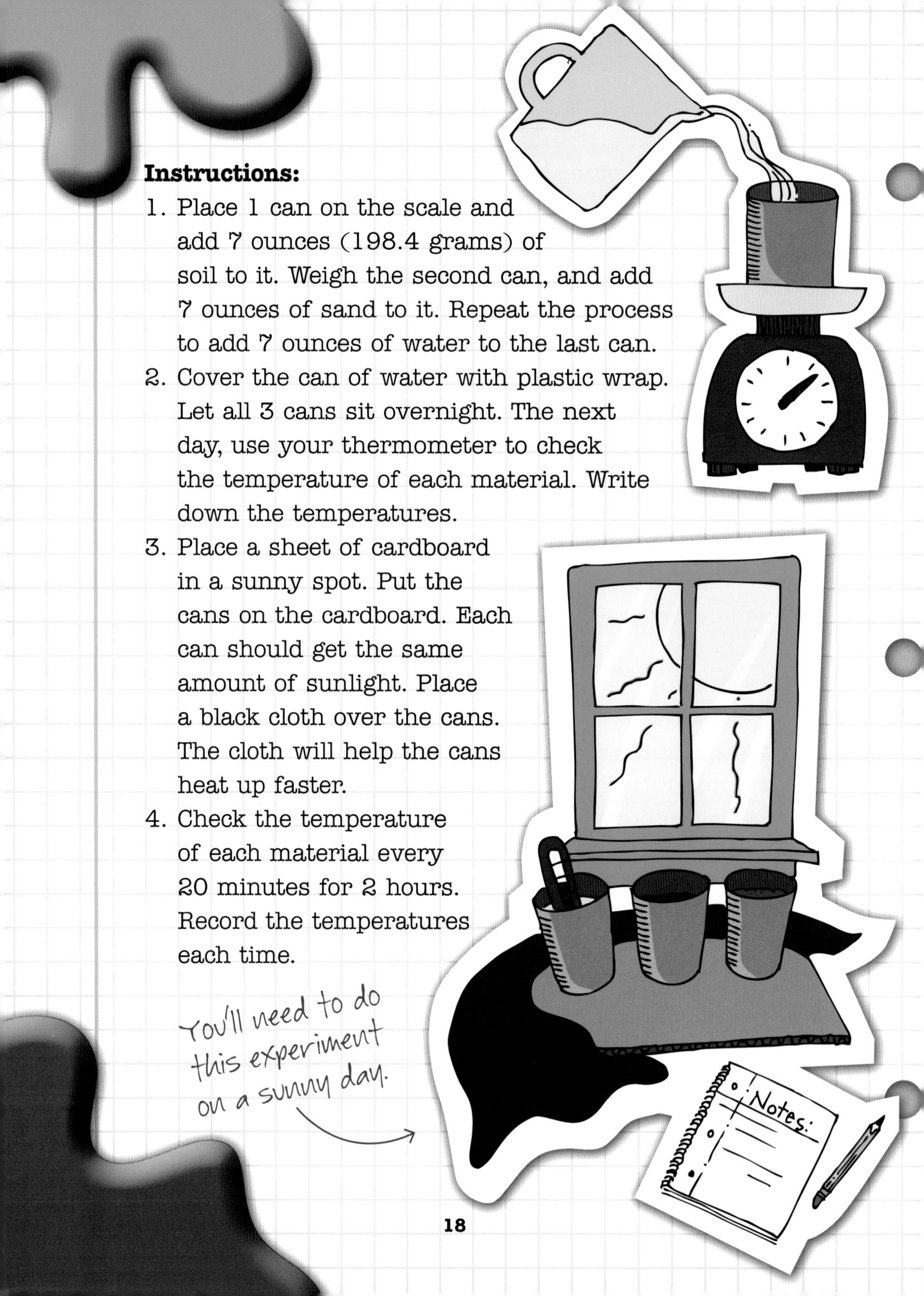

Instructions:

1. Place 1 can on the scale and add 7 ounces (198.4 grams) of soil to it. Weigh the second can, and add 7 ounces of sand to it. Repeat the process to add 7 ounces of water to the last can.
2. Cover the can of water with plastic wrap. Let all 3 cans sit overnight. The next day, use your thermometer to check the temperature of each material. Write down the temperatures.
3. Place a sheet of cardboard in a sunny spot. Put the cans on the cardboard. Each can should get the same amount of sunlight. Place a black cloth over the cans. The cloth will help the cans heat up faster.
4. Check the temperature of each material every 20 minutes for 2 hours. Record the temperatures each time.

You'll need to do this experiment on a sunny day.

5. Place the cans on a cookie sheet. Ask an adult to help you put the cookie sheet in an oven warmed to 120 degrees Fahrenheit (48.9 degrees Celsius). Leave the cans in the oven for 20 minutes. Have your adult helper take the cookie sheet and cans out of the oven. Carefully measure the temperature of each substance.
6. Use an oven mitt to place each can on a hot pad in a cool place.
7. Carefully record the temperature of each material every 20 minutes for 2 hours.

Conclusion:

Review your data. During Step #4, which material heats up the fastest? The slowest? During Step #7, which substance cools down the fastest? The slowest? Which material would you say heats up the slowest and cools down the slowest? This material best manages heat. It retains heat well and keeps temperatures more even than the other materials. Was it water? Was your hypothesis correct?

Experiment #4 Earth Is Constantly Changing

Lava shoots into the air during a volcanic eruption.

Earth's surface changes constantly. Volcanoes erupt. Large plates of rock below Earth's surface push mountains up out of the ground. Many other factors cause our planet to change.

Glaciers are large, thick masses of ice. Scientists know that glaciers covered many areas thousands of years ago. They carved and changed the land as they passed over it. How? Glaciers tend to pick up rocks as they slide along. Could this have something to do with a glacier's ability to carve Earth's surface? And what happens when a glacier melts? Come up with a hypothesis. Here is one option: **The ice and rocky material of a glacier can carve a landscape and deposit materials as it stops moving and melts.**

Here's what you'll need:

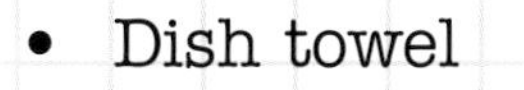

- Dish towel
- Sunny windowsill
- Ice cube
- Sand
- Flat bar of soap

You can model the action of a glacier with these simple materials.

Instructions:

1. Lay the dish towel on a sunny windowsill.
2. Dip one side of the ice cube in sand. That side should be covered well with sand.
3. Place the bar of soap on the towel.
4. Put the ice cube, sandy-side down, on the bar of soap. Press the ice cube down a little and slide it across the soap. How does this change the surface of the soap?
5. Dip the same side of the ice cube in the sand, to give it another coating.
6. Place the cube, sandy-side down, on the soap. Let the ice completely melt in the sun. Write down what you observe after the ice has melted.

Conclusion:

The bar of soap represents a landscape. The ice cube is a glacier. The sand represents the stones and earthy matter that glaciers collect as they move along. How did rubbing the ice affect the soap? Did it become rough or grooved? What does this tell us about how glaciers change land? What about when your mini-glacier melted? Did it deposit, or leave behind, earthy matter? In nature, glaciers are much heavier than your ice cube. Their weight also helps them dig into and scrape the surface. What would happen if you pushed the ice cube harder into the soap as you scraped? Try it. Was your hypothesis correct?

Volcanoes can quickly change the look of a landscape. A major volcanic eruption in the United States took place in Washington State on May 18, 1980. Mount Saint Helens erupted and swept away 250 homes, 47 bridges, and miles of railways and highways. The force of the explosion also removed 1,300 feet (396.2 meters) from the top of the mountain!

Experiment #5 Earth's Amazing Atmosphere

Earth's atmosphere is the layer of gases that wraps around our planet. The atmosphere is thick. It reaches more than 348 miles (560.1 km) from Earth's surface. Did you know that air has weight? A small amount of air may not weigh a lot. But the weight of lots of air adds up. For example, the air in a tall, thin column above a 1-inch (2.5 cm) square space weighs about 15 pounds (6.8 kilograms).

Spread atmospheric weight over a 2-inch (5.1 cm) square, and you now have 30 pounds (13.6 kg) of pressure. That's enough pressure to hold something in place when you want to move it. Could there be a way to visually demonstrate that air has weight? Could air pressure be used to actually help break something, such as a yardstick? Come up with a hypothesis. Here are two possible hypotheses:

Hypothesis #1: Atmospheric pressure is strong enough to hold a yardstick in place so you can break it.

Hypothesis #2: Atmospheric pressure is not strong enough to hold a yardstick in place so you can break it.

Here's what you'll need:

- Thin, lightweight, wooden yardstick
- Table
- Padded glove
- Safety goggles
- Sheet of newspaper

Great news! You don't need a lot of expensive equipment to do experiments.

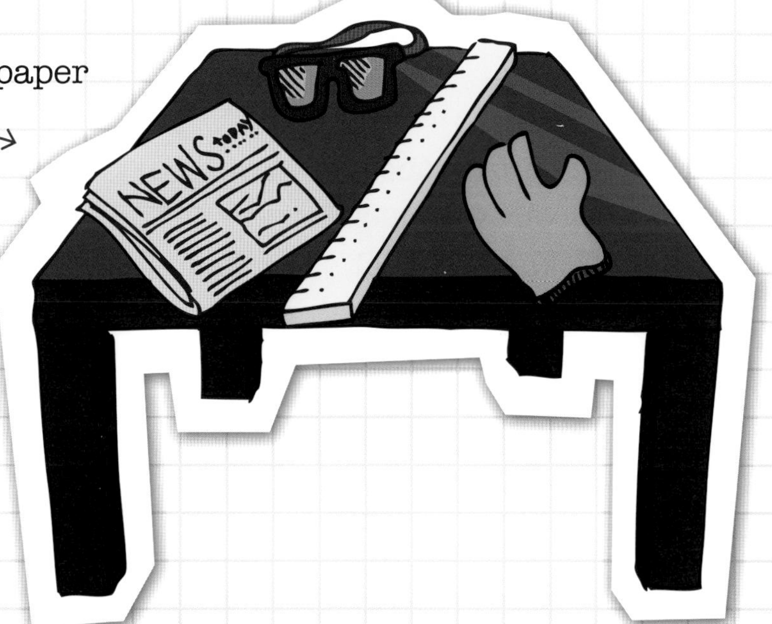

Instructions:

1. Place the yardstick on the table. Slightly less than half of it should extend beyond the edge of the table.

2. Put on the glove and safety goggles. Give the stick a quick karate chop with your hand near the end that's out in the open air. Make sure you are not standing in front of the stick when you strike it! What happens to the yardstick? Write down your observations.
3. Reposition the yardstick on the table in the same way as Step #1.
4. Open a full sheet of newspaper, and lay it over the yardstick. The crease should run along the length of the yardstick. Lay the paper evenly so it spreads out an equal distance over both sides of the stick. Smooth it down so that it hugs the table and yardstick and there are no air pockets.

5. Give the part of the yardstick that is sticking out in the open air another very quick karate chop with your gloved hand. What happens? Write down what you observe.

Conclusion:

Did the yardstick fly up the first time you struck it? How were your results different when the yardstick was covered by newspaper? Did it break?

By spreading the newspaper out, you created a wider area for atmospheric pressure to weigh down one end of the yardstick. The force of the weight of the air across all of the paper is strong. This extra downward force kept the end of the stick from lifting up as it did the first time you struck it. By chopping quickly, air couldn't slip in under the newspaper and help lift it. All of that atmospheric pressure was bearing down on the paper and on one end of the yardstick! That pressure on the newspaper was greater than the force of your blow to the other end of the stick. Does this explain your results? Was your hypothesis correct?

The air we breathe contains oxygen. You probably knew that. But did you know that it contains other gases? Air contains about 78 percent nitrogen, 21 percent oxygen, and 1 percent several other gases.

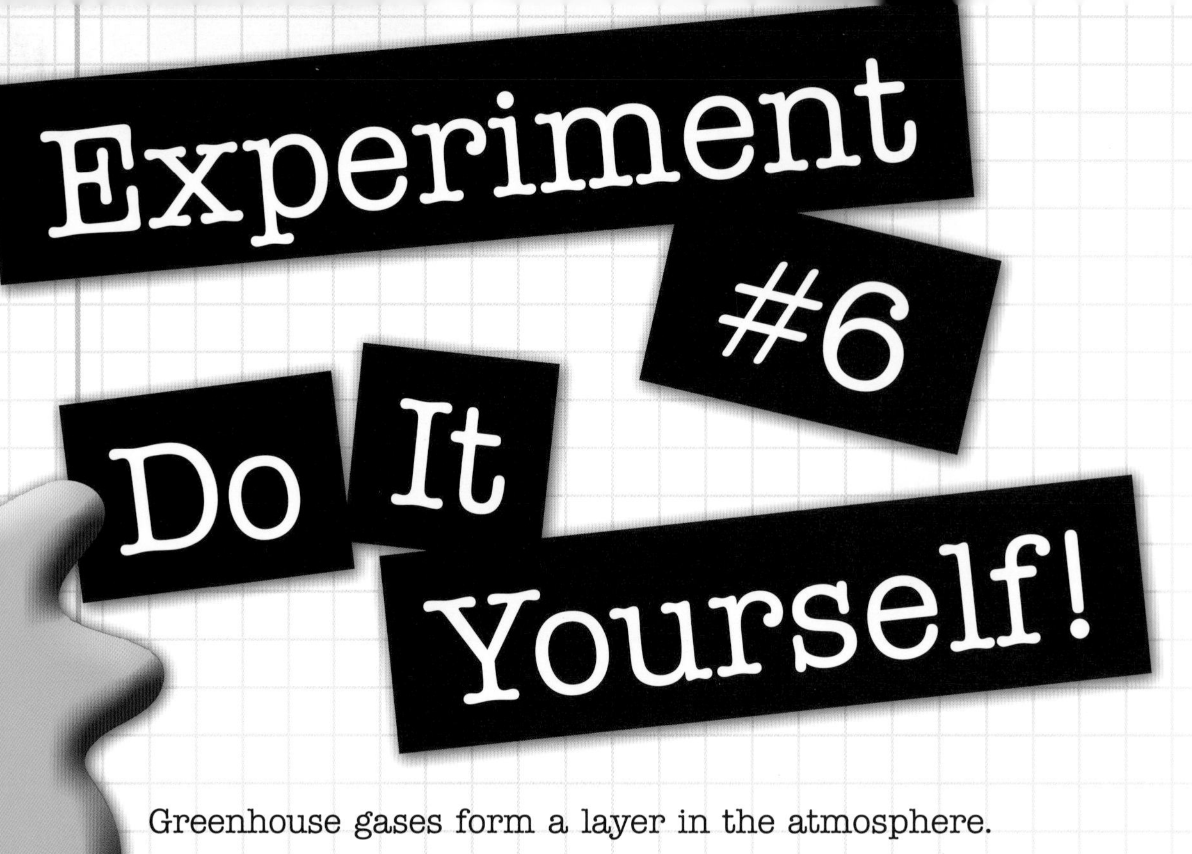

Greenhouse gases form a layer in the atmosphere. They trap heat. That's a good thing. Earth's surface would be much cooler without those gases. But burning fuels releases huge amounts of gas into the air. Many scientists believe this layer of gases is getting thicker and trapping more heat. These scientists point to an increase in these gases as one reason for a warming planet. How could you design an experiment about global warming and the greenhouse effect?

You could use two plastic containers with a thermometer in each. Cover one container with a tight layer of plastic wrap to represent a thicker "blanket" of gases. Leave the other uncovered. Do you think one container will get warmer in the sun? What hypothesis might you create? How would you test it? Give it a try!

Greenhouses are good for growing plants, but high levels of greenhouse gases aren't good for Earth's environment.

You've learned a lot about planet Earth. Pick one thing about Earth that interests you: plant life, the water cycle, ecosystems, weather, or any other topic. Then use your skills as a scientist to investigate. Planet Earth is waiting for your discoveries!

GLOSSARY

atmosphere (AT-muhss-fihr) the blanket of gases that surrounds a moon or planet

conclusion (kuhn-KLOO-zhuhn) a final decision, thought, or opinion

eclipse (i-KLIPS) the blocking from view of one object in space by another

gravity (GRAV-uh-tee) the force by which all objects in the universe are attracted to each other

greenhouse effect (GREEN-houss uh-FEKT) the warming of Earth's surface caused by gases that collect in the atmosphere and prevent the sun's heat from escaping

hypothesis (hy-POTH-uh-sihss) a logical guess about what will happen in an experiment

method (METH-uhd) a way of doing something

observations (ob-zur-VAY-shuhnz) things that are seen or noticed with one's senses

orbits (OR-bitss) travels around the sun or a planet

pressure (PRESH-ur) the force produced by pressing on something

FOR MORE INFORMATION

BOOKS

Gardner, Robert. *Earth-Shaking Science Projects about Planet Earth.* Berkeley Heights, NJ: Enslow, 2008.

Landau, Elaine. *Earth.* New York: Children's Press, 2008.

Williams, Zella. *Experiments about Planet Earth.* New York: PowerKids Press, 2007.

WEB SITES

EPA Environmental Kids Club—The Water Cycle
www.epa.gov/safewater/kids/flash/flash_watercycle.html
See the water cycle in action with this fun animation

NASA—It's a Breeze: How Air Pressure Affects You
kids.earth.nasa.gov/archive/air_pressure/index.html
For mini-experiments and information on air pressure

The Weather Channel Kids!—Global Warming
www.theweatherchannelkids.com/weather-ed/weather-encyclopedia/global-warming/
Learn more about global warming and its impact on the planet

INDEX

About the Author

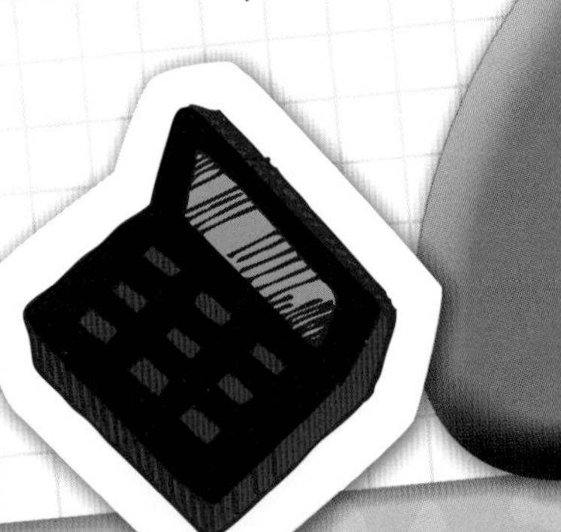

Matt Mullins holds a master's degree in the history of science. He lives in Madison, Wisconsin, but he hasn't always. When he was 14, he awoke one morning and saw everything outside covered in fine, gray ash. It was May 18, 1980. Mount Saint Helens, which was not even 35 miles (56.3 km) away, had just erupted.